T0368471

KINDERGARTEN...PLUS

OUTSIDE THE

FIRST GRADE

SECOND GRADE ETC..

AuthorHouse™
1663 Liberty Drive
Bloomington, IN 47403
www.authorhouse.com
Phone: 1 (800) 839-8640

Published by AuthorHouse 05/21/2015

ISBN: 978-1-5049-1125-2 (sc)
ISBN: 978-1-5049-0953-2 (e)

Library of Congress Control Number: 2015907458

Print information available on the last page.

Any people depicted in stock imagery provided by Thinkstock are models,
and such images are being used for illustrative purposes only.
Certain stock imagery © Thinkstock.

This book is printed on acid-free paper.

authorHOUSE®

Soar

As the Journey Continues

Patty Nelson, Author
Carolyn Smith, Illustrator

TABLE OF CONTENTS

Welcome to
Mrs. Nelson's Classroom

Great fun and teaching ideas for
Primary Grades K-1-2

Soaring in a Hot Air Balloon

For kids who want to learn more,
"Soaring in a Hot Air Balloon" for sure!
This book was created just for teachers and you!
So PEEK inside and take a LOOK!
We think your teachers will love this BOOK!
Learning new things like reading, writing and more!
Have fun on your journey learning to SOAR!

Pounds & incHes

School Scrapbook

Classroom Scrapbook

Students love to give their teachers artwork that they create at home. This is a great way to display their art work so all can see and enjoy.

During the school year, my students would proudly present me with pictures that they had created or colored at home. They were allowed to share them during "share time" and tell their classmates about the pictures that they had created or colored. The pictures would be hung in the classroom for the day and then placed on a page in our *"Kindergarten Class Scrapbook."* This scrapbook was placed on the activity table in our classroom so that when the students had time they could enjoy looking through it. This is a photo of our classroom scrapbook.

Creating a School Year Scrapbook

The primary grades are a very special time, since they are the first few years of children's public or private education away from their parents. This is a great time to create pages of their work in school and have them saved, put in scrapbooks, and given back at the end of the school year.

Students loved working throughout the school year on these pages. The students were told that these pages would be put into their school year scrapbook.

Have your students complete the following pages throughout the school year of events in which they will be involved. Pages included are handwriting, art, and worksheets from subjects taught. You can also include photos taken during the year by the teacher. These pages and photos are sent home to the volunteer scrapbook keeper, a parent, to be placed in each student's folder.

It was a very special last day of school when the students were given these scrapbooks. The parents were there for this end-of-the-school-year event. The parents, as well as their children, were amazed at the progress students made during the year. It was an exciting time for both parents and students to see such academic growth in these scrapbooks.

Following are some of the pages to be placed in each student's scrapbook. Also following are scrapbook cover choices; students may choose their favorite one to use.

Photos of Scrapbooks

Below are some of the scrapbook covers for Kindergarten and primary grades. They were laminated on a colored sheet of 9" x 12" paper. The scrapbooks were bound together by parent volunteers using our school's binding machine. The pages were placed in the order that they were created throughout the school year. It is a wonderful keepsake for both students and parents.

Scrapbook of School Memories

My School Year Scrapbook

Name_____ Date_____

School_____

My School Year Scrapbook

Name _____ Date _____

School _____

My Kindergarten Scrapbook

Name _____ Date _____

School _____

Kindergarten Scrapbook

Name_____ Date_____

School_____

Monthly Art for the School Year Scrapbook

Covers pages for the students' scrapbooks should be mounted on a piece of colored construction paper. If your school has a laminating machine, it is nice to have the front and back covers laminated.

Following the cover pages are pages labeled for each month of the school year. They are to be handed to the students during the month labeled at the top of the page. Instruct the students to create a picture, using their crayons, depicting something that represents that particular month. After students have completed their drawings collect their illustrations for that particular month and send the drawings home with the scrapbook volunteer's child. The parent will file the artwork in each student's folder in the order that it was received. Folders labeled with each student's name are included in the scrapbook keeper's box and sent home at the beginning of the school year.

Also, added to the school year scrapbook are some daily class assignments, including handwriting, number writing, stories, art work, etc. Remember to date these pages as well before sending them to the scrapbook keeper (or have a volunteer date the pages). If the school has a binding machine, have a parent volunteer bind each student's work, including the front and back covers, at the end of the school year. This makes a wonderful keepsake of that school year for parents and students.

January

February

March

April

May

June

July

August

September

October

November

December

TO BE YOU!

I want to
teach my students to be
Amazing...Prepared...Ready!
TO NOTICE
Be Responsible
Kind and Gentle
Enthusiastic and Confident
To learn how to think
and be an EXCELLENT YOU!
It's your life to live.
I'm honored to be a part of your beginnings...
etching our time together in your and my memories!

WHEN YOU FALL SOARING IS POSSIBLE!

iMAGINATION

ENTHUSIASM...CONFIDENCE ME & TO
TO BE
LEARN HOW TO THINK... YOU! EXCELLENT

I LOVED MY JOB...
MY CLASSROOM...
THE PARENTS

THE JOURNEY
KEEPS GOING...BEYOND
MY CLASSROOM...

First Day of School

Class Photo

Last Week of School

Class Photo

First Name Writing on The First Day of School

*
Keep for the end of the School Year's Scrapbook.

Last Name Writing on the Last Day of School

* Keep for the end of the School Year's Scrapbook.

First Number Writing
And
A-B-C's

I LOVE WRITING NUMBERS and aBC'S... IT'S SO MUCH FUN!

Beginning of the School Year

Last Number Writing
And
A-B-C's

End of School Year

Number Practice

Beginning of the School Year

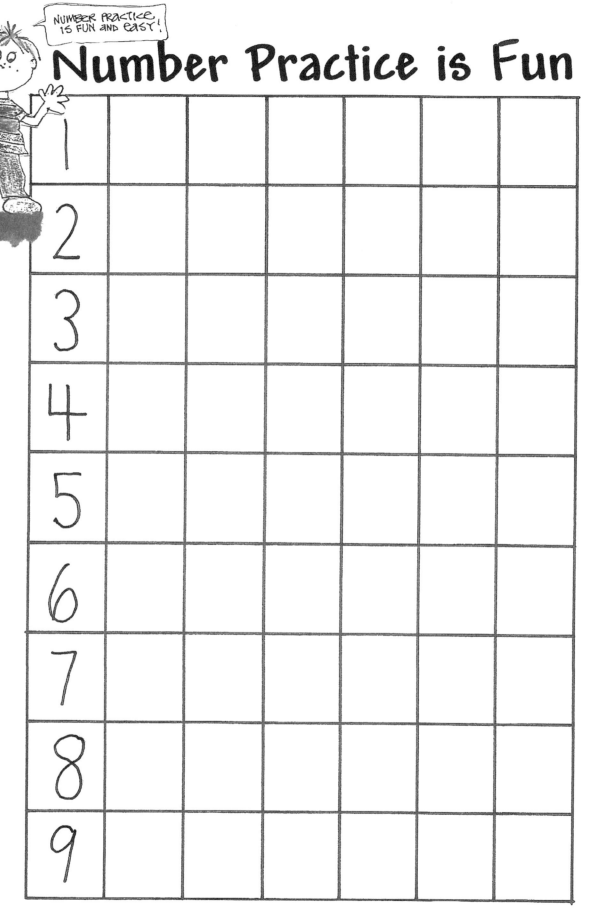

Number Practice is Fun

NUMBER PRACTICE IS FUN AND EASY!

1
2
3
4
5
6
7
8
9

End of the School Year

36

Self Portrait

Beginning of School Year

Self Portrait

End of School Year

Height and Weight

Weight _____

Height _____

Beginning of the School

Height and Weight

Weight_____
Height_____

End of the School Year

Height and Weight

Weight_____

Height_____

Beginning of the School Year

Height and Weight

Weight _____

Height _____

End of the School Year

Alphabet Art Fun

Upper and Lower Case

The following pages are illustrations for creating art using upper and lower case alphabet letters! This is a fun way to recognize and learn the name of each letter and the sound the letter makes.

Have fun creating alphabet art together as a class. Demonstrate step by step on the chalk board while the students observe you, follow your directions, and draw on their own paper. As you and your students draw, emphasize the sounds of each letter, including the long and short vowel sounds.

Creating art involving a correctly formed letter, while also learning the sound, was lots of fun. This was my students' favorite skill to do during our phonics time.

Another possibility is to purchase *Time to Draw!* by Frank Webb. It can be purchased at Teachers Exchange of San Francisco, 600 35th Ave., San Francisco, CA 94121 (1974 Frank Webb).

Alphabet Fun

Capital Letters

A	B	C	D	E
F	G	H	I	J
K	L	M	N	O
P	Q	R	S	T
U	V	W	X	Y
Z				

Alphabet Fun

Lower Case Letters

a	b	c	d	e
f	g	h	i	j
k	l	m	n	o
p	q	r	s	t
u	v	w	x	y
z				

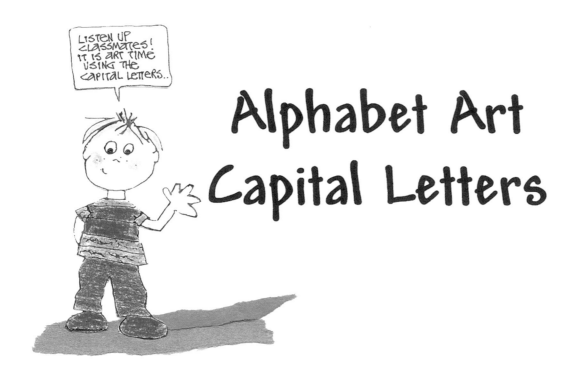

Alphabet Art
Capital Letters

Beginning of the School Year

Alphabet Art
Capital Letters

End of the School Year

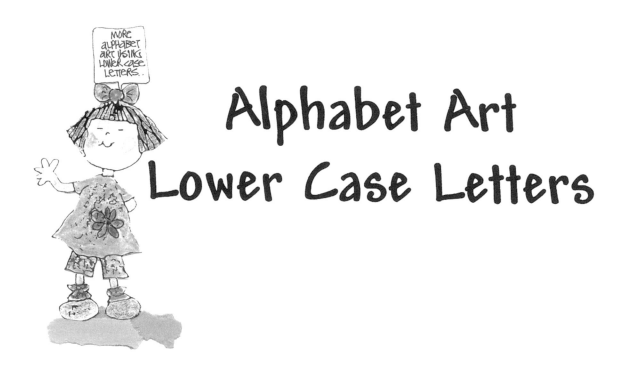

Alphabet Art
Lower Case Letters

Beginning of the School Year

Alphabet Art
Lower Case Letters

End of the School Year

# My Handprint

My Family

Autographs
of my
Classmates

My
Students'
Autographs

At the end of the school year I had my students sign
their autograph for my personal teaching scrapbook.
The "Autographs of my Classmates" page goes into
the student's scrapbook.

My Own
Scrapbook Creation of
my Favorite Day at
School

Last Day of School
Program

from the mouTains to The Prairies to the ocEans wHitE with foam... god bLess America mY hOMe sweet Home...

57

Last Day of School Program

On the last day of school, the parents were invited to come to our classroom. I talked a little about the school year and the academic skills that their children had accomplished. I also discussed the plays presented, our senior citizen project, and other fun learning activities.

When the parents entered the classroom, an art display was there for them to enjoy. The students had painted ceramic pieces fired in a kiln. The art pieces were each displayed on a piece of typing paper with the student's name on it. The students were instructed to take their ceramic piece home after their parents completed the test that was going to be given.

Before the test, the students were presented with their scrapbooks. The scrapbooks contained schoolwork and art pages that they had completed during the school year.

Then I told the parents that their children wanted to "test them" on what their children had learned during the school year. The students and I created the "test questions." We had fun reminiscing about our school year together as we created the questions for the parents.

The parents' names were drawn in no particular order for them to come forward with their student. The parent drew the question out of the box and handed it to their student. Along with my help reading the question, their child repeated it for their parent(s) to answer. The parents were told that if they did not know the answer, they could use their lifeline, which was their child! Everyone in attendance had a wonderful time. Cookies and punch were served.

What a fun way to end my eighteen years of teaching kindergarten. It was hard to say good-bye and leave such a wonderful career. I have such fond memories of teaching in Sedona, Arizona. I had the privilege of mentoring the young teacher who is now in my classroom and knowing that she enjoys using many of my ideas. My hope is that you will also find the ideas in this book fun and exciting for your students. The photo below, with my husband, was taken in my kindergarten classroom on my last school day.

~Fun and Memorable~
School Year

Happy and yet sad faces all wrapped up into one
important last day of a great school year!

Our School's Kindergarten Club

Always look at the bright side of teaching even when it gets overwhelming sometimes.

Kindergarten Club

The kindergarten club at our school started when the first class of kindergarteners enrolled at our new school was being promoted to the high school. In order to become a member of the kindergarten club, a student must have entered on the first day of kindergarten and remained a student at our school until the last day of their eighth grade.

It was a way to highlight those students who remained at our school throughout their elementary and middle school years. They were given a medal as a remembrance of their time at our school.

The last evening of their school day, there was a promotion program. Several of the students being promoted spoke of their time and fun memories of their elementary school days. Then each student who was eligible received a Kindergarten club medal. It was a truly fun way to send my Kindergarteners off to high school.

This is a photo of one of my Kindergarten students who was being promoted that evening. She sent me this photo of the two of us. It now has a place in my book as a remembrance of how wonderful and rewarding it is to be a teacher.

My memories of teaching Kindergarten will never be forgotten. This book will always be a reminder of the fun days I had "setting the stage" for eighteen years teaching darling Kindergarten children in Sedona, Arizona. I still keep in touch with many of these students and their parents. It was deeply rewarding for me to be a part of their lives.

My hope is that this book will benefit those who also have the opportunity of teaching students in their first year of public education. It is a privilege to "set the stage" for young students to enjoy being in school and help them acquire the love of learning.

OH BOY!
I am NOW an OFFICIAL
MEMBER
OF THE
KINDERGARTEN
CLUB.

Mrs. Nelson
Kinder Club
Lifetime
President
XXO
Your Students

66

Words are powerful, choose
your words carefully.

Teacher's Rewards

10
9
8
6 7
5
3 4
2
1

68

HOP SCOTCH

Dear Mrs. Nelson, Aug. 2013

Thank you so much for all the years of newspaper clipping and sweet notes! I loved getting them! ♡ Thank you for always being so supportive and for being the best kindergarden teacher ever!

Love,

Never waste a moment to tell a student how important they are to you.

A Teacher's Reward

The note below was from a former kindergarten student of mine written to me just prior to his High School Graduation.

May, 2011

Dear Mrs. Nelson,

Thank you for letting me have one of the best Kindergarten years of anybody's life. I still remember the alphabet books we did, where for every letter we would write an animal with the letter it started with. I keep reflecting on those days and really miss nap-time, even though I hardly slept then. I remember just about every game we would play at recess, especially when we would try to dig to China. Then came the Kindergarten club at the 8th grade graduation, and now, very soon I am graduating High School. Still throughout High School you always sent a picture of me everytime I was in the paper. So over all these years I just want to thank you for everything.

Love,

I REALLY LIKED MY K-TEACHER! I AM GOING TO WRITE HER A LETTER WHEN I GET BIG!

A Teacher's Reward

The letter below is also from a former Kindergartener who is now pursuing her career. How rewarding to keep in contract with former Kindergartens of mine.

WOW! HERE'S ANOTHER ONE OF MY TEACHER'S REWARDS..

April 7, 2012

Dear Mrs. Nelson,

Thank you so much for the letter! It _did_ make its way to me, & was such a wonderful surprise for me to find in my mailbox - truly brightened up my day!

I did have a great time in New York with my campers, & I'm having a great time here in Milwaukee doing some really wonderful theater. I've enclosed some pictures from some of the past season's shows so you can have a look at what I've been doing - I hope you like them! Love,

Students' Memories

(A Teacher's Reward)

During each school year, one of the most rewarding and exciting things I did with my students was having them present plays to their parents in our classroom.

Then, since they truly loved performing, they were brave enough to want to include the entire school and our community at the end of the school year. The performances were presented on the stage in our school's auditorium.

At the beginning of the school year, our first play ("Mother Goose Rhymes") was presented in the classroom using the microphone. As you might expect, this was a big hit with all the children and their parents. Even the students who were very shy were eager to enter into this fun and new experience. After that, they were excited to move on to the school's stage and perform for the student body, parents, and community members.

The following plays were performed on the school's stage:

> *Christmas Play* (December)
> *Patriotic Program* (February)
> Various end-of-the-school-year plays
>   (for example *Charlotte's Web* and
>   *The Little Engine that Could*)

By the end of the school year, students were very comfortable memorizing their parts, speaking into a microphone, and being part of a class production. One kindergartener even sang the "The Star-Spangled Banner" in our patriotic play held on the stage.

Near the end of the school year, I read *Charlotte's Web* to the entire class. All my students thoroughly enjoyed it, and they wanted to present it as a play for the entire student body of our school. We did just that, and of course there were many proud parents, to say the least, as well as the teacher!

Making lasting memories of their school year is important for the students. Having fun and enjoying learning both seem especially important so during this initial phase of their education. That is why I think Kindergarten is one of the most important school years for a child.

On a following page is a drawing one of my students gave me after playing the part of Charlotte in the story of *Charlotte's Web*. She created it for me, as a gift, in the eighth grade as part of a booklet that my former kindergarten students made when being promoted into high school.

Have fun with your students, and create kindergarten memories that they will never forget—and probably you won't either.

"What a wonderful and
rewarding school year!
I truly love working
with my students and helping
them to become
what they are capable of being."

Charlotte's Web

Author E.B. White

Drawing below created by a Kindergarten student
playing the part of "Charlotte" in our class play.

Gift
From a Parent
Volunteer

Teacher Gift
created by a parent

Paddington Bear comes to our classroom after reading the story Paddington's Holiday Fun

by Michael Bond"

~ A gift from one of my students for our classroom ~

Gift from
Dr. Nancy Alexander,
Sedona Oak Creek School
District Superintendent
Sedona, Arizona
upon my retirement day

(photo of the plaque)

Kindergarten Class

I LOVED WORKING IN MY LETTERBOOK.

Above is the photo of <u>my last kindergarten class on the first day of school</u>. Standing in front of our class bulletin board which displays their self-portrait creations. Each student is proudly holding the first letter-book in the series of <u>"Beginning to Read, Write and Listen."</u> This reading curriculum used at our school for kindergarteners is an outstanding reading program.

Kindergarten Class

This photo of my last Kindergarten class was taken at the end of the school year and just before my retirement. Every Kindergarten student of mine, still enrolled at our school, came through my classroom to say goodbye on my last day of teaching. It was a very rewarding day for me after teaching for eighteen years in Sedona, Arizona. I truly enjoyed by teaching days in my Kindergarten classroom.

What a great school year we had
~Hopping~
~Jumping~
~Climbing~
~Soaring~
through these books having lots of
fun learning and
making wonderful memories!

May 29, 2003

Dear Parents,

It is hard to believe that this school year is now history. It has been a very rewarding year for me and I hope for your child. The children have worked hard this year and have accomplished much. I am proud of the progress that they have made.

It is always with mixed emotions that I close a school year (especially this one as I will not be returning in the fall) and release my little kindergarten friends into the care of another teacher.However attending Big Park School, I know that they will be in good hands!

I thank God that I have had the opportunity to get to know your family and to be a part of your child's life. Have a wonderful summer.

Sincerely,
Patty Nelson

Kindergarten Friends Forever!

Codi and Sophie

My hope for you is that this
series of books that my
sister-in-law and I created
helps you to make learning fun
and meaningful
while creating wonderful
memories for your students and
yourself as you
journey through
the school year together!

Sincerely,
Patty Nelson

Welcome to
Mrs. Nelson's Classroom
"Great Fun and Teaching Series"

Hop on the Bus
Climb Aboard the Train
Jump in the Wagon
Soar in a Hot Air Balloon
...as the "K-1-2 Journey" begins!

A great teaching series of four books
full of unique ideas and fun
for teachers and their eager students!

Author – Patty Nelson, Sedona, Arizona
Illustrator. – Carolyn Smith, Colorado

Printed in the United States
By Bookmasters